ACED

*Superior Interview Skills to Gain an
Unfair Advantage to Land Your Dream Job!*

Gerald Ratigan, CMA, CPA

This book is dedicated to my amazingly supportive, smart, beautiful, encouraging, flexible and loving wife Amanda. She is my perfect life partner and I couldn't have accomplished this goal without her.

And, to my high-energy, inquisitive, canny and vocal son Anders. I love you both always and forever.

ACKNOWLEDGEMENTS

THIS BOOK HAS been over a decade in the making. I've always felt the need to share my experiences and help guide others to master the job search process. I would like to especially thank my family, friends, mentors and coaches for their endless support and specific knowledge. Without a loyal team I would not have been able to hit publish.

I've dreamed of becoming an author FOR YEARS, and it wasn't until I joined Self-Publishing School that the dream came true.

I'm now am on the path to becoming a BESTSELLER, and I know EXACTLY what to do! Not only do I know how to publish my first book, but I can also build it into a business.

It doesn't matter if you can't write, have no time, or no idea you CAN become a bestselling author, and Self-Publishing School WILL WORK for you.

Don't wait. WATCH THE FREE VIDEO SERIES NOW:

www.AcedInterview.com/selfpublish

TESTIMONIALS—Amazon Verified Purchases

"I found number of useful tips in this book. The book helps you organize your thoughts. The section on how to behave, sit, and body positions during the interview were interesting. I found this book useful to get myself prepared." - #1 Hall of Fame Top 10 Amazon Reviewer

"Aced is the kind of book I needed. The level of detail included in the book, made me think of some new ideas to implement. The nine success tips were helpful, and the two closing questions will definitely be utilized. The chapter on technology and the shift to online interviews was timely and had some great tips. This is an important book for anyone job hunting, as well as, anyone looking to move up the ranks within their current job." – Current job seeker

"Consider this book your critical, go-to tool to ACE the interview and WIN your dream job! You're prepared and rehearsed for the BIG interview for your dream job. You're nervous, but you think you aced it. Then you wait, and wait...and wait some more. And eventually hear that they hired someone else. But WHY? I've been through this painful process, as you probably have too (as has just about everyone who strives for bigger and better) and, frankly, it cuts you deep.

Worst of all is you just know you could have won that opportunity...if only. Here is wise and perceptive job-hunting warrior and self-confessed hirer to explain exactly what to do and what NOT to do to ACE the interview and win the job you really want. My only regret that this book comes towards the end point of my career - it would have made a huge difference earlier on.

But for anyone just graduating, career-changing, moving on, moving up, downsized, discouraged, wanting more and knowing they deserve it, this is the basic how-to manual to getting there. Highly recommended for anyone in the job market who needs the tools to ace the interview and win the job of their dreams. This should be on the must-read list of anyone just graduating or trying to navigate a tough job market and needing the wise counsel of someone who's been there, navigated that, and come out a winner." – Seasoned Professional

"Employed or Unemployed... You need to read this book. ACED is for you if you are looking for a better position or if you are unemployed and want to get hired quickly. It's much more than just a book on interviewing. It contains an easy-to-follow, step-by-step blueprint for landing your dream job, as well as a resources section with a link to free bonuses. If you want a better job, get this book, read it, and implement the advice. You'll be glad you did." – Professional Career Coach

CLAIM YOUR SPECTACULARLY AWESOME FREE GIFTS FOR BUYING ACED!

I sincerely thank you for purchasing ACED and helping me become a #1 Amazon best seller! As a huge thank you, I have created valuable gifts just for you.

To obtain your FREE Audiobook and FREE Salary Negotiation Resource Guide ($39 value) today, please go to:

www.AcedInterview.com/bonus

Table of Contents

Obtain your FREE Audiobook and FREE Salary Negotiation Resource Guide ($39 value) today, please go to:

www.AcedInterview.com/bonus

INTRODUCTION

INTERVIEWING IS NOTORIOUSLY difficult. But, this book will make you a better interviewer.

After reading this book, you'll soon be able to build immediate trust, credibility, and authority with your interviewers. You will possess more confidence and be more authentic. You'll be prepared and in control like never before—even if you're reserved, quiet, or shy.

Mastering Interview Skills to Land Your Dream Job Is within Your Reach!

This is the single most important book for you to land your dream job. Because I have been where you are and understand what you are going through, I have the solution to help you nail interviews and change your career for the better.

The truth is that nobody wants to be an average job interviewee. You, especially, don't want to be average because being average won't get you your dream job.

But you're NOT average. You can land your dream job. But how?

Imagine how your career could be different if you knew exactly what you needed to do in your most important interviews every single time. That's exactly what I'll show you how to do.

Learn from an Expert Who Cares about You and Your Future!

Now you may have been disappointed in the past from other so-called coaches or experts and nothing seemed to work. I understand you may have tried other training programs and read other books before. Luckily, I am not that person, and this is not that book. I'm not going to disappoint you and let you down like previous experts might have.

Why am I different?

In this book, I share my decades of experience as both a job candidate and as a hiring manager. Over my career, I've interviewed well over 50 times across all levels within an organization. I've also interviewed hundreds of job candidates over the years to fill positions in my organization and on my team.

I hold the unofficial record for most jobs as a professional based on my current number of years' experience. This has allowed me to create and learn from a diversified, world-class global business experience. I've worked for numerous accounting firms and public companies, both large and small, from Miami, Florida; to Houston, Texas; to Melbourne, Australia; back to Miami; and now Dallas, Texas. I've worked in departments from external audit, to internal audit, to financial reporting, to controllership and back.

I am a CPA, CMA, and corporate finance executive for a public company with international operations. I've worked at the BIG 4 public accounting firms and many blue chip companies across the globe. I want you to land your dream job and achieve all your career dreams!

I've helped so many professionals all across the world—and now it's your turn.

Research Shows—Action Takers Have the Most Successful Careers!

While this book is your opportunity to land your dream job, you must be committed to transforming your career fortunes and making a huge, measurable impact during your next interview. To land that job, you must be willing to work for it.

I know that you often think about who you are and what you have to offer your potential employers. And that's why you've got to take the next step in pursuit of interview mastery right now because before you know it, this opportunity will have disappeared and your competition will be offered your job . . . Your Dream Job! It's your choice.

You may be a recent grad, a seasoned professional, or somewhere in between. No matter where you are in your career, the insider secrets I share in this book will help you ace your next interview and gain an unfair advantage over your competition.

So what can you do to ensure you have a great interview?

Master Aced. Superior Interview Skills to Gain an Unfair Advantage to Land Your Dream Job!—helping you give IMPACT interview responses instead of just "answers." When you do, you'll win praise from your interviewers and receive that dream job offer!

While everybody wants to be the best at interviewing, only a few are committed to making rapid, measurable changes. Are you?

Without Massive Action and Change NOTHING WILL CHANGE!

Look, the way I see it, you have a choice. You can either coast through life, without a plan, without the help of an expert coach, or you can commit to achieving interview success with a simple step-by-step guide to land your dream job!

How do you want your interviews to be remembered? As somebody who communicated exceptionally; or as somebody who was just like everybody else; or worse yet, the smallest version of yourself, missing out on yet another job opportunity.

I want you to do a little exercise with me right now. Think of the last interview you were on. How did you react when the interviewer was talking to you? What were you thinking? How were you feeling? Did you get the job offer?

I hope you felt absolutely confident and had a positive mindset the entire time. Unfortunately, job seekers often get derailed at the first instance of challenge and controversy. When interview questions increase in difficulty, I've seen candidate's confidence wane. Shortly thereafter the interviewee is completely derailed. In your last interview, if this was you, it is ok. But, I don't want this situation to happen to you again.

How would you like to have the confidence of knowing exactly how to prepare for your dream interview? Surprisingly, these skills can be taught. There are specific techniques—from creating your unique selling proposition, to identifying ideal employers, to connecting with your interviewer on a sub-conscious level, to using emotional intelligence—that will make your interview memorable. And I've got a personalized plan for you to make that happen in this book as I provide relevant skills to be successful.

So whether you're just starting your career or you're a seasoned professional, if you're not getting multiple job offers every single time you interview, and/or if you're meeting resistance when you try to explain your experience, then this book is exactly what you need.

The book includes . . .

- Pre-interview tactics and preparation tips to boost your confidence during the interview. They're the key to being ready to impress your interviewers at the right times. A significant part of the work of a remarkable interview is done well before the interview. That's what will make your interview memorable. And . . . let me key you in on a little-known secret: running through your interview in your head for the first time in the car on the way to the interview is NOT preparation.

- Items you must be prepared for to prevent any unnecessary stress that may derail your positive mindset on the day of your interview(s).

- New ways to answer interview questions and body language tactics that help build a deeper connection with your interviewer.

- Techniques to master the online interview. There's a big difference in the way that they're structured.

- Secrets to maximizing your salary and other compensation through advanced negotiations.

- Networking tips to help you find your dream job.

- Tips to overcoming an imperfect resume or dealing with job search fatigue.

- Fundamentals of impromptu speaking so you can handle any interview question that's thrown at you.

- Advanced tips on what to wear to maintain a credible appearance to ensure confidence and limit your day of interview stress.

What Other Are Saying . . .

"This book is a must-have for anyone looking for a job. It does not only talk about key interview skills, but it shows the insider tips that can get you into the interview room. It is full of practical ideas on how to land your dream job."

"I just started reading ACED and it is absolutely captivating. Amazing guidance to land your dream job."

"I finished reading the book . . . I like the step-by-step approach you used, and you covered topics like interviewing online that I haven't seen covered before. I will use this as a tool for helping others since I get lots of women who talk to me about dissatisfaction in their jobs . . ."

Now Is the Time for You to Land Your Dream Job!

So what are you waiting for? Now is your time. Your time for interview mastery. Your time to take control of the next step in your career. If you want all of those things . . . and a whole lot more, then you just need to read this book so scroll back up and click the download button.

CHAPTER 1

How to Find Your Dream Job

"All our dreams can come true,
if we have the courage to pursue them."

—*Walt Disney*

JOB SEARCHING: A confusing and downright scary subject for most job seekers. During this time, job seekers face this task wondering where to begin and whom to contact.

Getting started can seem daunting, but it helps to follow the advice, start with the end in mind. After conducting well over 50 job searches at different times in my career, I have learned the importance of following that tip. To do this, ask yourself when you think about your ultimate dream job at the height of your career, what title do you picture yourself having? Are you a CEO, CFO, President, Director, Partner, or maybe a Manager, Supervisor, or Teacher? No matter what the position, you need to have a focus.

Having a focus provides you with a target and will allow you to pursue a specific path forward. Without a clear direction and defined goal you are at significant risk of wandering aimlessly throughout your career. For me, I've always dreamed of being a CFO. Once I had this role identified, I could reverse engineer the career path to this job.

I then worked backwards to research the types of positions that were usually promoted to CFO: typically the Controller or VP of Finance. Then, I moved down another level to the roles right under these positions: Assistant Controller, Senior Manager, Senior Analysts and many more. I repeated this step over and over until I moved down to my current level. After doing this, I knew where to focus my time and energy, seeking only positions on the path to my dream job.

Step 1: IDENTIFY YOUR DREAM JOB

So, now it's time for you to determine your dream job. What is the title? Once you know your dream job, go through the same exercise I went through, working backwards at each and every level. With a clear understanding of the types of roles you need to achieve to work up to your dream job.

Take a few minutes now and list below at least three titles of jobs that you currently believe to be your ultimate dream job.

_____

_____

_____

You can now begin your research to reverse engineer your own defined career path. The big question is where to go from here. In the age of mass information, it is too easy to get distracted by any and all job advertisements. The majority of which, won't be relevant for you and are nothing more than a waste of your valuable time. It is essential to identify job opportunities that match your skills, expertise, and career trajectory.

Step 2: LEVERAGE YOUR CURRENT NETWORK

There is tremendous value in the connections you have already established. Don't make the common mistake of overlooking your existing personal relationships. You may be afraid to ask for help or assume the other person won't be interested in helping you. If you are about to enter the job market or looking to begin a career change, it is all right to let your friends, family, and other relationships know you are looking for opportunities to land your dream job.

Now, for those of you just starting your career, my #1 tip to increase the probability of job search success is to allocate sufficient time to networking. For those of you who are seasoned professionals, I hope this isn't the first time you've heard this, but if it is, or you just have not focused on external relationship building, then the good news is you still have time.

You will need to dedicate time, energy, and resources to develop and nurture professional relationships. If you heed this advice, you will be two to three steps ahead of everyone else competing with you to land your dream job. This doesn't mean if you don't have a robust network you will not be successful in your job search; it will just take more time.

Take a few minutes now and list below the names and contact details for at least three relationships of people that you know that work at companies or know people that work at companies where your ultimate dream job could take place.

_____

_____

_____

_____

_____

Now that you've identified a few individuals that could have a direct impact on helping you obtain your dream job, you goal is to enhance each relationship. Within the next 24 hours you should call or email them to reconnect and share something of value. This could be as easy as providing a recent article that relates to a specific issue they are dealing with. The more creative you are, the faster your relationship capital will be built.

Step 3: MASTER THE ONLINE SEARCH

Job search engines, company websites and online job boards are all potential options for you to locate your dream job. However, these sources should be considered cold leads because you don't have a direct relationship to provide you with a personal introduction or recommendation. Of course, landing a job through this method is not impossible; however, it is significantly more challenging.

From my experience online job applications can become a time consuming process. If you apply to numerous jobs, it is likely you will eventually feel overwhelmed. Many companies have very exhaustive online application processes requiring you to manually input every job you have ever had along with other personal information. Be prepared to spend up to an hour filling out each application. And on top of that, you should tailor your resume for each and every application. I've debated with myself whether making the process more efficient would be in any company's best interest. However, the alternative viewpoint is only serious applicants would spend that much time to complete the entire process.

To get you started looking for jobs online, I have listed below a few job search websites I have used in the past. You may find them useful as you begin your dream job search process.

- www.Indeed.com

- www.CareerBuilder.com

- www.TheLadders.com

- www.Monster.com

Step 4: BUILD A PERSONALIZED DREAM JOB SEARCH TEAM

Recruiting firms are specialized resources that are available to you during your job search. However, not all recruiters are the same. There are recruiters that specialize in specific industries, geographic locations and even level of experience within an organization. So you need to ensure your masterful secret search agent is worth your time and energy. So, how can you identify the right recruiter for you?

I highly recommended you log into www.LinkedIn.com and search for a few recruiters that you can meet in person. When you find someone that you feel may be a good fit, you should send them a personal message that you are starting your job search process and would be interested to learn more about their services. Once you have connected, then your next step should be to schedule an interview with them.

Do take your interview with a recruiter very seriously! It is during this meeting they are evaluating you to determine how comfortable they are presenting you to their clients. If you don't make a great impression with your recruiter it is very unlikely they will submit you to interview and you risk missing out on landing your dream job.

It is helpful to understand that recruiters are not all the same. First, there are recruiters who work internally for a company. They may or may not receive a commission for job placements. They may be full-time or part-time, and they do have goals to bring in a certain number of candidates and get the job filled in a certain period of time.

Usually larger companies have the resources to have an in-house recruiting department. In my experience, these companies do not allow resumes to be submitted unsolicited by recruiters as they will not pay the placement fees.

The second category of recruiters are those whom the company has specifically partnered with to fill a position. This is called a retained search. In this scenario, a company may not have the resources to have an internal recruiting department. They then will have one recruiting firm serve as their HR and recruiting department to screen applicants on their behalf. What normally happens is the recruiting firm will negotiate first with the company, and then begin marketing the role to candidates.

So when you work with a recruiter, ask him or her if this is a retained search and if they have an exclusive agreement with the company within the first few minutes of the recruiter selling you on the position. This single question will help you determine how much leverage he or she possess in the process. Ideally, he or she is performing a retained search.

The third category of recruiters are what I call Agents to the Masses. The industry term for this category is performing a contingent fee search. The recruiter will only earn a fee from placing a candidate at a company. These recruiters may or may not have an existing agreement in place for their placement fees at a specific company. The more established and larger recruiting firms usually have already negotiated their placement fees with companies so they possess a competitive advantage over firms that do not.

I have landed many jobs both using and not using recruiters. Surprisingly though, I have always engaged a recruiter in each job search. I'll be honest, I've had both very positive and negative experiences using recruiters. First and foremost, the way to guarantee success is to make sure the recruiter is completely objective and has your best interest in mind. Unfortunately, like any sales focused industry, some recruiters are only concerned with the commission that they will make by placing you.

Earlier in my career before I learned the insider secrets to the recruiting industry, I had an especially bad experience. I had a recruiter who I thought was retained by a company I was very interested in working for. However, when I was in the final negotiation stages, believing the process would be complete within hours, the process dragged on for multiple days. I was left in the dark and had no idea what was going on. I had another offer as a plan B and was now strongly considering accepting that offer. While it ultimately worked out with the first company, I learned that the recruiter was negotiating his fees with the company at the same time as me. If I had been more educated on the different types of recruiters, I could have avoided this situation.

In general, the more resources you have working for you the better. I recommend using two or three different Agents to the Masses recruiters. By using only one recruiter, you are limited to only his or her network and knowledge of current job openings. From my experience, having two recruiters allows you to double your market for potential jobs and also mitigates your risk if your first recruiter has performance issues. When beginning a job search process, you should interview multiple recruiters to make sure that you're comfortable with them and ensure that they're credible in the market. You don't want to find yourself locked into a recruiter who does not have an extensive network of key relationships with the companies that you want to work for.

Think of the recruitment industry as being similar to real estate. Imagine for a moment that you're buying a house. If you're working exclusively with one agent, you want to ensure that that agent has a widespread network and that he or she has tremendous experience. Unfortunately, if you're working with an inexperienced agent that doesn't know the market or doesn't have negotiation experience, his or her short-comings could break your deal and make your purchasing process miserable.

To increase the probability of landing your dream job, interview many recruiters. When you find a great match, your job search process will become much more productive!

Network Like There Is No Tomorrow. And the Earlier in Your Career the Better.

The most successful job seekers are forward thinkers who put forth effort into developing a long-term network building strategy. I can hear some of you asking, "How can I build a new relationship?" An easy first step is to reach out to your college or university alumni. Are you involved in their local chapters? Are you involved in their online groups on Facebook or LinkedIn? If you aren't, after finishing this chapter, you should go online and search for your college or university and join their alumni groups. Not only should you join, but you should add value. Introduce yourself and then spend time learning the key topics the group values, and begin commenting with your valuable insights.

Depending on your area of expertise, take action by sharing something that you've seen in the news recently that impacts companies you want to work for. This tactic helps you gain exposure. By being active and providing consistent value, you get your name out to future employers and begin establishing your authority, credibility, and trust. From there, you can begin to expand your network from your college or university to trade associations or other interest groups with members who are likely to be future hiring managers.

Are you beginning to get new ideas of where you can start connecting more?

Another consideration is joining and participating in professional organizations. As an accounting and finance professional, my experience with several professional organizations (The Institute of management Accountants, Sarbanes Oxley and Internal Controls Professionals Group, SEC Professionals etc.) was critical for achieving my high career trajectory. You may be asking why this is important. It matters because even at a senior executive level, I must continue to build my network and exposure to enhance my ability to land my dream job.

With all this time spent networking, you may think I am superhuman or have more hours in a day than you, but you'd be mistaken. I have a young child at home, love to travel, and hold regular speaking engagements to train young professionals. My secret is that over time, I've become extremely productive by significantly reducing distractions and by leveraging relationships and activities. I'm not special; these are learned skills through years of practice and mentoring.

If you want to grow your career, you should become active in and take leadership roles within new organizations. By just showing up and being disciplined in creating value, over time you will increase your expert status, become an authentic leader, and be known as a leader in your field. So after you have joined your university group online, research and join one trade association or special interest group. Remember to share your key insights and provide solutions.

You should also join Toastmasters, a valuable group for all job seekers. Joining this organization will help you build your leadership and communication skills, and help you connect with other professionals that also value personal development. You can find a chapter in almost every city around the world. A unique benefit to joining Toastmasters is the opportunity to connect with people from different professions at different stages in their career. You can take advantage of their absolutely priceless networking opportunities for a very nominal membership fee. Visit www.toastmasters.org to learn more.

List the names of at least three organizations that may be a good fit for you to join:

_____

_____

_____

_____

_____

If you implement this guidance and become active in a few new groups, then you're guaranteed to establish relationships that will have a positive impact on landing your dream job! So now I hope you understand the more people you can connect with, the greater the chances are that someone in your network can help you land your dream job.

Don't forget to obtain your FREE Audiobook and FREE Salary Negotiation Resource Guide ($39 value) today, please go to:

www.AcedInterview.com/bonus

CHAPTER 2

The Secret to Gain Your Unfair Advantage . . . Technology!

"Leveraging the latest technology resources to enhance your competitiveness during a job search is mission critical to landing your DREAM JOB."

– Gerald Ratigan, CMA, CPA

THE JOB SEARCH process has evolved remarkably in the past few years. You can now apply to work for a company anywhere in the world, right from the cozy confines of your living room. And to go one step further, you can complete the interview process almost completely online.

So while technology is providing job seekers with more access to amazing opportunities, the job search process has not been made easier. It is actually becoming more difficult. Not only are you now competing with other job applicants from other cities and states, but also from countries all across the world. And, to make the process even more challenging, there are an overwhelming number of job websites and postings that take so much time to filter through.

So what can you do to make yourself stand out from your competition for your dream job and utilize technology to give you an unfair advantage?

First, you should always be weary of sharing your personal information on the internet because not all recruiting websites and job boards guarantee privacy. Unfortunately, I learned this lesson the hard way. As a young professional, I wanted to set the world on fire, so I jumped right into looking for jobs using the internet.

I shared my resume and personal contact information on a handful of websites. Immediately after submitting my resume, I started getting non-stop phone calls and emails. At first I thought this was amazing. However, almost all of the calls and emails were for direct sales jobs that were absolutely not relevant to me.

After two weeks of borderline harassment, I had to change my phone number and set up a new email. I recommend if you haven't already, to establish a professional email address. For example use firstnamelastname@gmail.com.

CREATE AN ONLINE PROFILE

With that being said, you should use technology to build an online profile that highlights your career experience and help recruiters and companies find you. Have you heard of LinkedIn? Do you have a Linkedin profile? If not, you should. According to LinkedIn's most recent About Us information, the Company reports over 467 million registered users world-wide, growing almost 20% when compared to the prior year. Additionally, of the current registered users, only 29% are users from the United States. What do these metrics and trend mean? Should you be concerned? Absolutely.

I shared the latest LinkedIn stats to bring awareness of the global competition you now face as you attempt to land your dream job. The trend is crystal clear. We now have a global economy where employers can source employees from almost any country. And even more distressing, it is now easier for your competition to create their own online profile and compete directly with you.

Now is the time for those of you who do not have a LinkedIn profile to take a break, a short break from reading the rest of this book, and go online to www.LinkedIn.com. Once you register, set up a profile with a professional picture and start populating your profile with what you would typically have on your resume.

If you want to see an example profile, have a look at mine at www.LinkedIn.com/in/JerryRatigan. Then feel free to add me as a connection as I'd love to answer any additional LinkedIn or job search questions you may have.

For any skeptics out there whom I haven't convinced yet, I can confirm LinkedIn is the primary research tool HR staff, recruiters, and hiring managers use to run initial screening and background checks on potential employees. These companies want to obtain social proof of your experience, credibility, and past performance. These searches are performed during the application process to make sure there are no red flags. As a hiring manager for many companies, I would always search LinkedIn to learn more about the candidate than what was disclosed on his or her resume. Red flags are never deal breakers, only an opportunity for the company to learn more from the applicant during the interview.

STREAMLINE YOUR JOB SEARCH PROCESS

LinkedIn users also have an advantage over other job seekers because they have access to a robust and active job board. Now that you have an account, you have the ability to search for jobs specific to geographic regions, titles, companies, and the most recently posted positions. You can even set up a specific search and receive notifications for when new jobs are posted that meet your specific criteria. I recommend you perform a few job searches and test out the job search intelligence you now have at your fingertips.

These search results will provide you with a summary of people in your network that work for the company. You can also use LinkedIn to help you become a private investigator to learn more about a potential employer's culture. Through your search, you can see how many recommend the company, how many recommend the key employees who work there, and even learn about your potential manager.

By having a LinkedIn profile, you can build a massive network of professionals who may be able to introduce you to a hiring manager or HR department. In my opinion, most people want to help their connections to find a job and will make the introduction if asked. However, they need to feel comfortable that the person they are recommending is someone they like and trust. They don't want to risk damaging their credibility. This is the reason why connections matter. Having LinkedIn connections matter.

Being connected to someone in a company and even to a person currently working in a department of your dream job is of immense value. I can't stress enough that being able to build, nurture, and leverage professional relationships will be a critical factor in your success. Linkedin makes this process manageable so take advantage of their resources.

So, it is important to start building LinkedIn connections. This process of online networking is similar to the process I shared in the previous chapter to help you network in person. Begin with those whom you already know, work with, have worked with, and do business with. Many of these individuals are probably on LinkedIn and would welcome a connection request. Next, join at least two LinkedIn groups in subject areas you want to gain additional knowledge in. Join the group or send a join request if the group is restricted. Over time, these routines, if practiced regularly, will help you build a strong network of key professional relationships to help you ultimately land your dream job.

List of Groups that you have interest in joining:

NOT ALL JOBS ARE EXTERNALLY MARKETED

Most government and government supplier companies are required to publically post job openings. However, for other companies, there is a high volume of job openings you will never see. Why? Many companies will perform an internal search to fill a position. Then, they may use a retained search, which often times is confidential. How then are you supposed to know if your dream job comes available in either of these situations?

Think of your job search like finding a house in the real estate industry. Certain houses may be sold pre-market and may never make it to a MLS listing. A house may put up for sale, but is being shopped behind the scenes by real estate agents who are picking up the phone and calling their top potential buyers.

These top agents have a backlog of buyers who are interested in certain properties, and this is where they find out from their colleagues that this property is going on the market. They'll call and test the interest in that property, and then it's sold before it even hits the MLS listing. You want to be notified about your dream house, or should I say dream job, becoming available. By creating a profile on Linkedin, you now put yourself in position to be easily found and contacted directly by companies and recruiters that are looking to hire their next superstar.

A word of warning for anyone who has gone through a few job searches: if you are currently employed, do not post on Facebook or LinkedIn that you are looking for a job. Unfortunately, I see more and more young professionals make this mistake. You do not want to put yourself at risk of being fired or terminated by your current employer before you have another job lined up. If your employer finds out, then you'll likely end up in HR with some explaining to do. Do proceed with caution.

EFFECTIVELY TRACK YOUR APPLICATIONS

Along with utilizing online job boards, you can use technology to help you keep track of your applications. As you start progressing through your job search process and you begin to build momentum with many potential dream jobs, it is important to keep track of your application status. You should keep an up to date schedule of all the companies and positions you are applying to. In this schedule, you should track key information such as application date, resume file and location, application progress, existing connections you have to the company, and any other intelligence you've gathered in the process.

Technology advancements are allowing job seekers across the globe more opportunities to land their dream job. It is now up to you to leverage your new found knowledge to position yourself for job search success.

SPECIAL reminder......claim your FREE Audiobook and FREE Salary Negotiation Resource Guide ($39 value) today, please go to:

www.AcedInterview.com/bonus

CHAPTER 3

Overcoming the Imperfect Resume

*"Hardships often prepare ordinary people
for an extraordinary destiny."*

—*C.S. Lewis.*

EVERYONE KNOWS CLIMBING the world's largest mountain requires an expert guide. And if you have an imperfect resume, you have a big mountain to climb as you try to reach your career summit. I can be your expert guide because I, too, have had an imperfect resume: I come across on paper as a job hopper.

Over my career, I've made many attempts to climb my Career Mount Everest, despite my imperfect resume, and I have learned the critical lessons needed for success. At this point in my career, I have worked for almost ten different companies and in two different countries, the U.S. and Australia. Each career move was a calculated career move to acquire new skills and experiences. Unfortunately, this strategy, while advancing my skill set, has at times flagged me as a job hopper.

From experience, the job search process is at least twice as difficult and requires more effort if you don't have a perfect resume. Blemishes such as long gaps, a high volume of jobs, and/or legal issues are just a few red flags that often scare off potential employers. Don't be completely discouraged though if your resume is less than perfect; you can overcome this challenge.

Recently, I found inspiration in a fortune cookie: "life is more difficult near the summit." This quote can have a positive impact on your mindset. Think of your current status of your dream job search process as if you are climbing a mountain. Some of you may feel as if you are climbing Mount Everest. Take a moment to pause and reflect on the significant progress you have made. You may not realize how very close you are to achieving your ultimate goal. The summit is right before you. To reach the peak though, you need additional perseverance and some timely insider secrets.

Throughout my numerous job searches I have faced many challenges: I did not possess the required experience; I changed jobs too often; the companies I've worked for weren't in the right industry or size. Have you heard these same comments or something similar? Whenever I faced those brick walls, I had to step back and rethink my job search strategy. Every time I got knocked down and rejected, I was forced to rethink how I positioned myself.

Through facing these challenges, I learned to overcome my resume's imperfections. You too can overcome blemishes on your record or experience based on past mistakes or gaps in your resume. If you are attempting to make a career change, you can do it even if your previous experience and education doesn't perfectly align with the roles that you're seeking out.

DEALING WITH BLEMISHES ON YOUR RECORD OR EXPERIENCE

You can address these issues in your cover letter. Additionally, consider bringing it up in the interview first before the interviewer asks. This is an advanced negotiation skill where you are in control of how this information is presented. By addressing the elephant in the room, you disarm any personal reservations you subconsciously hold. Alternatively, it could be something the interviewer has in the back of his or her mind, and unless you address it, he or she may not be able to get over it.

The best advice in all your communications is to be honest and transparent. Explain the situation. If you made a mistake, explain you made a mistake, but you learned from it. That's the point that you want to spend more time on. Go into more details on the lessons you learned. What do you know now that you wish you would have back then? You want to keep the focus on establishing that you're a different person now and you've taken steps to improve yourself. You should explicitly guarantee that those same mistakes won't happen again. These responses will help your prospective employer overcome their initial reservations.

Please take the time before you start any job search process to remove any self-created blemishes. By that, you should perform an external, unbiased review of all your social media accounts—Facebook, LinkedIn, Twitter, Instagram—and delete posts and pictures that would create some unnecessary questions about your character. Depending on the severity of your posts, pictures, and overall profile, it may be best if you delete the profile in its entirety.

It is all right to start a new profile or account to prevent any misconceptions that a prospective employer would hold against causing him or her to pass your resume by. As a tip to ensure you stay proactive in managing your social media presence, do not press send without asking "Would I be comfortable with this being shown on the cover of the Wall Street Journal? Or being sent directly to my boss or client?" If not, delete it.

OVERCOME EMPLOYMENT GAPS

Generally speaking, employment gaps of one or two months are normal and expected. Most recruiters and hiring managers will not identify this length of gap in work experience as an issue. However, if you have a gap that is three months or longer, you will need to spend more time crafting interview responses that provide more details concerning your extended break in employment. Make sure your explanations are credible and thorough to address the interviewer's concerns.

You should take the same approach when dealing with resume blemishes: explain it in your cover letter and address it during the interview. You want to explain the situation that caused you to end your previous employment. Do provide enough details so the interviewer has no objection to hiring you. In the event you were terminated, share your lessons learned and how those experiences will help you in the job you are interviewing for. Be prepared as there is a high probability everyone you interview with will ask you about it. You want to make sure you have your story memorized, and you are clear and confident in your responses.

HOW TO MAKE A CAREER CHANGE

You may have gone to school, graduated, and pursued a career that someone recommended or you thought would be the right fit for you. Unfortunately, after a few years working in that industry, it just was not resonating with your passion. If you find yourself in this situation, it's going to be a bit more of a challenge for you to get past the initial rounds in the interview process. To be successful in your job search, you will have to rely more heavily on your network if you don't want to start over at entry level positions. You should also volunteer for organizations that can help you develop experiences and transferable skills—communication, cultural awareness, change management etc.—which will help you be successful in a new career.

If you can obtain these important skills, then your chances of success increase dramatically. Possessing these valuable skills may help a prospective employer overlook any other skills or experience gap you may have.

So rest assured, you can overcome the imperfect resume; it is all about open, honest communication; addressing it first yourself; and gaining valuable skills which help you shine despite any resume flaws.

CHAPTER 4

Advanced Interview Preparation and Interview Question Insights

*"Whenever you are asked if you
can do a job, tell them, CERTAINLY I CAN!
Then get busy and find out how to do it."*

—*President Theodore Roosevelt.*

ALMOST EVERY INTERVIEW follows the same process. And not every phase of the process is the same. The more advanced knowledge and insights you have on what phase you are in, the more likely you will be prepared to land your dream job.

THE FIRST INTERVIEW

Your first interview will most likely be the HR screening interview. Congratulations, if you've gotten to this part, you've made it through the first stage of the Land Your Dream Job process. It is during this interview where the company makes an additional effort to screen out candidates that may have great resumes but don't meet other specifications.

Be mindful that the interviewer works in the HR department and may not be an expert in the technical department you are being interviewed for. Additionally, it is unlikely that they are familiar with the day-to-day responsibilities of the specific job you are interviewing for. Therefore, your focus should be on sharing your work experiences which demonstrate you have met all of the job requirements listed in the job description.

BEHAVIORAL INTERVIEWS

After the HR screening interview, you will have behavioral interviews with the hiring manager and a few other managers in their department. You may even interview with their boss. During these interviews, you can expect the questions to focus on your historical work experiences in an effort to understand your background and experience to determine if you are the right fit for the job.

No matter who your interviewer is, the first question you will be asked will be, "Tell me about yourself." Your answer to these four words will set you up for success if you answer spectacularly. You definitely should memorize your response to this question and practice it over and over again. By starting the interview off with a strong and powerful response, it will give the interviewer comfort and confidence in your communication skills. It also will positively influence his or her first judgment over whether or not you're a right fit for the role.

For this question and all others, you should stick to two or three minutes to give an answer. During your interview preparation, set a timer as you practice to ensure you do not let yourself ramble. You don't want to go on and on and talk about lots of experiences that are not relevant to the position you are interviewing for. As you craft your answer, make sure you share a story or two about how you've overcome challenges to the best of your ability and how you achieved tremendous results. And, of course, how you could do the same for this company.

The second question you are almost guaranteed to be asked is 'Why are you looking for a job?" This question is asked whether or not you reached out and applied to the company or through a recruiter, or if the company contacted you directly. It is this question that often trips up interviewees as they have not spent enough time preparing for this specific question. I think most job applicants assume the company knows why they are looking for a job so they do not expect to be asked. However, not providing a well-thought out and authentic response to this question may lead to trouble.

I have provided a list of additional behavioral questions you can expect to be asked during your dream job interview. For each item I have provided insights to why the company will ask this question.

1. Tell me about a time you had to work with a team.

The company wants to learn about your collaborative skills. Are you a person that can be immediately inserted into a working team and contribute from day one?

2. Tell me about a time you had to overcome an obstacle.

In this question, the interviewer is testing the level of adversity you have faced and your ability to handle stress. You may want to address this question with a specific project you worked on with a tight deadline.

3. Tell me about a time you had to change plans or strategy when working toward a goal.

Decision making is one of the most important skills employers are hiring for. This question allows the interviewer to learn about how you process risks and rate your project management ability.

4. Tell me about a time you had to work with other departments.

Without communication skills, a professional will not advance in their career. Being able to effectively communicate across departments and seniority levels is crucial to success. Using this question, interviewers want to learn about your experience level and how confident you are talking with, emailing and presenting to others in their organization.

5. Tell me about a time you had to deal with a difficult colleague.

The work environment can be tumultuous at times, especially when critical deadlines are at risk of being missed. This question probes your conflict resolution skills as a leader. The interviewer wants to understand from your perspective how you address a negative situation of having a colleague create problems for you or your team.

6. What is your career goal? Where do you see yourself in 5 years?

Normally, one of the last questions you can expect to be asked is about how your short and medium term career outlook. The interviewer is interested in learning your personal assessment of self-worth and how ambitious you are in your career. I recommend as part of your research that you identify a position in the company at least two levels above the role you are interviewing for.

My favorite quote of all time is "The true measure of a person is determined not during times of comfort and convenience, but instead during times of challenge and controversy," by Dr. Martin Luther King Jr. The best job candidates are those that can handle the pressure of being challenged during the interview. In this chapter I've shared with you valuable knowledge that will prepare you to overcome challenges and have a great interview.

CHAPTER 5

Day of the Interview:
Before the Start

"Success doesn't come to you, you go to it."

—*Marva Collins*

WHAT MOST INTERVIEWEES don't understand is often times they are the ones that prevent themselves from landing their dream job. Over the course of my career, I've learned how to get myself in the best mindset to prevent any self-imposed obstacles on the day of my interview. And, I'm going to share them with you.

DRESS TO IMPRESS

Your looks matter, so dress to impress. What you wear makes the first impression to your interviewer. Of course, you should make sure you look professional and competent in order to set the right tone from the onset of the interview. However, on top of that, dressing professionally will add to your confidence. When you feel good about yourself, you are more likely to be in an extraordinary state of mind, positively impacting your performance.

In your preparation, make sure you know the companies culture to avoid being under dressed or overdressed. Based on your research, you should be familiar with their norms and expectations. If you are interviewing for accounting or finance roles, I recommend you dress conservatively. If you are in sales and marketing then there is no reason to go too conservative. No matter the department you are hiring for, to reduce the stress during the day of the interview, set out your clothes the night before. Any steps you can take to limit the decisions you have to make before the interview, the better.

ARRIVE ON TIME

Imagine you're in the reception area, waiting to interview for your dream job. What time did you arrive? Were you there the moment that your interview was scheduled to begin? If the interview starts at 9:00 a.m., did you walk out of the elevator exactly at 9:00 or were you there a few minutes early? One secret to success is based on a saying that I learned years ago in band camp. The band director started every rehearsal with the following saying that I'll never forget.

"To be early is to be on time. To be on time is to be late."

Think about this saying for a moment. Your first interview of the day could be the one that matters the most. Don't risk being late. You don't want to have a 9:00 interview, and run out of that elevator at 9:00 or 9:05 because you'll feel flustered and won't have the resolve to get that offer because your mind may be flustered. Also, when you're late, the interviewers will think you are not punctual or responsible, and that you do not value the interviewer's time.

As a hiring manager, if the candidate does not respect my time, I worry they will not be reliable in meeting deadlines. So remember, to be on time for your interview means to be early, but how early is early? A good rule of thumb is to arrive between five and ten minutes early. No less and no more. Anything more than ten minutes and you risk looking unscheduled. You may even create unnecessary stress on the interviewer as he or she may make an attempt to re-shuffle his or her schedule.

What if you do arrive more than ten minutes early? Don't wait in the reception area. If you are very early, 30 minutes or more, I would find a local McDonald's or Starbucks. Use this extra time to review your resume one final time. But, be mindful of the time, so you leave for your interview with at least 15 minutes to spare so you don't risk being late.

If you arrive at the interview 10–30 minutes early, and there isn't a coffee shop nearby, then I recommend you park in the back of the company's parking lot. This way you can complete you final preparations in your vehicle and not worry that you might be seen. Then with about 10 minutes to the start of the interview, start walking to the building so you can arrive at reception with five minutes to spare.

What if you are running late? I highly discourage this behavior; however, I understand, and most interviewers do recognize, that some situations are outside of your control. Whatever you do, do not blame traffic as that excuse will not be viewed kindly by your interviewers. In very rare circumstances, I have been late because of an unscheduled work meeting which ran late. In these situations I have let the interviewer know that. If you are going to be more than ten minutes late, I would make an attempt to reschedule the interview.

You need to plan your time accordingly to get there on time. The time of day of your interview will determine how much time you need to allocate for your journey. Is your interview at the beginning or end of the day? Rush hour will definitely add commute time. Give yourself a minimum of thirty minutes to locate the office and navigate parking because you want to allocate time for unexpected traffic.

I hope it is common sense to use Google maps, MapQuest, and/or the Waze app. Plot your course the night before, especially where you will park! Also, don't hesitate to call the company's HR department or reception to get clarification on the location and parking situation. Do they have a specific parking lot? Will they reimburse your cost? These are all issues you should resolve before the day of your interview.

If you are cutting it close to being late to your interview, then park in the nearest available location to the company's office and pay the extra parking fee. Unfortunately, parking lots are not always easily identifiable, especially in downtown urban settings as it is easy to confuse one lot for another. You'd be surprised the number of job candidates who were late to an interview because they couldn't find parking. So factor in time to deal with potential parking issues.

SUPER DUPER SECRET TIP

Use the bathroom in the lobby of the building, not in the office of the company you are interviewing for. This expert advice gives you a safer environment to adjust your clothes, perform any needed deep breathing exercises, and to give yourself positive self-talk. It would be slightly awkward if you were talking to yourself in the stall next to someone who ends up interviewing you. He or she just might have a different opinion of you after that unusual situation. You've been warned.

DON'T LET OTHERS RUIN YOUR MOOD

Have you ever experienced completely clueless drivers who are unaware of their environment and aren't paying attention to what is going on around them? Years ago, I was interviewing at a company, and as I was pulling into the parking lot, a driver flew right through a stop sign and almost side swiped me. I was enraged! My blood immediately boiled, and I was ready to honk my horn and cause a big scene. Instead, I took a deep breath and decided not to let this situation put me in a sour mood, as I was super excited about acing my interview.

Interestingly, in that moment, I had a decision to make. To let that driver knock me out of my positive frame of mind or to choose not to be bothered and instead move forward. In my head, I told myself he was just rushing to make a critical meeting to help calm me down.

Surprisingly, the last interview that day was with a senior executive of the company. As I walked into his office and introduced myself, I realized he was the superb driver I met earlier in the parking lot. He was completely unaware of the situation that occurred. Had I escalated that issue, there was no way I'd have any chance of surviving the interview.

OBSERVE THE CULTURE

You will have many opportunities to observe the company's culture to determine if it is the right fit for you. As you are sitting in reception waiting to interview, watch the employees going in and out of the area. How are they behaving? What are their mannerisms and expressions? When they pass by their colleagues, do they appear to be happy to be there? Or, are they reserved and quiet, not acknowledging others as they walk by. You should continue to observe the culture during the entire time you are on-site to obtain a glimpse of what it would be like to work there.

ONCE YOUR NAME IS CALLED

You will be met at reception by either an HR representative or your first interviewer. The clock starts now for you to make a great impression. You will want to ensure you demonstrate great behaviors of a future employee: likability, loyalty, and dedication.

Recent studies have concluded that interviewers make a decision in that first 90 seconds whether you're the right candidate for the role. If this is the case, it reinforces my earlier point of timeliness. If you show up to the interview late, you're already at a significant disadvantage at making a great first impression. I would even go so far as to say if you show up late, it's almost guaranteed that you will not receive a job offer.

CHAPTER 6

Trust Is a Must!

"Every experience in your life is being orchestrated to teach you something you need to know to move forward."

—*Brian Tracy.*

IF YOU BUILD immediate trust with your interviewer, you will jump light years ahead of your competition. If you don't, you risk being passed over and letting your competition land your dream job.

Knowing this can give you anxiety. Early in my career, when I would think about my upcoming interviews and the people I'd be meeting for the first time, I would experience self-doubt. However, I knew in order to build a successful career, I would have to overcome these fears and become skilled at building connections. Over time, I learned that trust had to be established immediately upon meeting someone for the very first time. Earn the interviewer's trust by leveraging your vast and unique life experiences.

PREPARE WITH PURPOSE

Think of your interview as a special project requiring a tremendous amount of research. It is necessary to not just be prepared, but to be prepared with the right type of research. In order to make you stand out from your competition well before the interview, you need to research and obtain a list of names and titles of the people you will be meeting with. Once you have this information, you need to use LinkedIn to gain as much insight and reference material as you can for each person. If you are working with a recruiter, a top notch recruiter will have performed some of the research for you and will provide you with links to your interviewers' social media profiles.

During the preparation phase, I normally scan each person's LinkedIn profile, spending 15 minutes on each profile. I would then take a few minutes to check out any of their other social media accounts—Facebook or Twitter. While checking these profiles, I mainly focus on their work experience, special accomplishments, and discovering if we share any connections or friends.

It would be to your advantage to learn that your interviewer used to work at your current place of employment or at a company your friends or family work for. Maybe your interviewer was an alumnus of your college. Or they volunteer at an organization that supports a cause you are passionate about. Knowing this information beforehand is extremely valuable.

Along with researching the interviewers, you also need to research information about the company. Check out the company's social media sites, and go to www.GlassDoor.com to check out what current and former employees have to say about the company. If the company is a public company, you should also review their latest U.S. Securities and Exchange Commission filings via www.sec.gov. On this website, you can learn about major new contracts, debt obligations, and other information that may be just the right information you can bring up during your interview. By completing this type of expert level research you are guaranteed to WOW your interviewer.

The information gained in this step of the interview process is the foundation for the overall interview. All the intelligence that you obtain in this process can be used to tailor your responses and questions during the interview. In isolation, this component will not guarantee interview success. However, if you are unprepared and show up to the interview without an already robust knowledge base of your interviewers and company, you won't be as comfortable and confident as you have the potential to be.

BREATHE MAGNIFICENTLY

Having sufficient breath is another simple yet underutilized interview success skill. During your interview, you must be able to clearly and confidently articulate your answers, making the case that you are the right fit for the position. Making sure you have a full breath at the beginning of each response helps give you increased confidence and power.

This will give you a better chance at meeting your objective because you can communicate more clearly. A full breath will also provide you the opportunity to use more vocals to vary your responses. This will prevent you from sounding boring and will keep your interviewers interested and engaged during the entire interview.

I'll be honest. At first, I was very skeptical of breathing techniques having any meaningful impact. I then became a passionate supporter of meditation and yoga. After taking a few classes I've been converted. I've since made an effort to attend at least one yoga class a week. Your breathing is very important to your overall energy levels, helping you achieve peak performance. Being calm and leveraging your breath can be a useful asset during times of intense stress.

Let's try an exercise to ensure you are always speaking confidently using your breath. For those of you that practice yoga, this is something that should come easy to you. If you are unfamiliar with yoga, that shouldn't deter you. I only recently became exposed to yoga and its benefits to improve breathing to reduce stress and achieve full energy.

Begin by first blowing out all the air that you have in your lungs. Yes, blow it all out. Now, give your answer to the common question, "Tell me about yourself." Start right away without taking another breath. How did you do? How would your interviewer rate you? Were you feeble and underwhelming? Now I want you to answer that same question, but this time, I want you to take a full deep diaphragm breath. Breathe in through your nose and feel your diaphragm expanding. Once you've taken a full breath, I want you to answer that same question. Now how did that feel? What was the difference between those two responses? I believe with 99.9% certainty that the second answer, the one with the full diaphragm breath, was powerful and authoritative.

You need to make sure that with each and every response, you're taking a full breath. Remember to take your time when the interviewer asks his or her question. First, pause and take a full breath before responding. By controlling your breathing, you can control your thoughts and emotions. Breathing magnificently gives you additional time to gather your thoughts. This helps to ensure that you are thinking before you speak. And when you do speak, you speak with confidence.

YOUR SPECTACULARLY AWESOME ELEVATOR SPEECH

It is critical that you have a well-rehearsed elevator speech. It must be a clear and concise introduction and overview of your unique selling proposition. Wait, I hear you saying, but I'm not a salesperson. I hate selling. Unfortunately, the interview process is definitely a major sale because the product is YOU!

Taking a more strategic approach will help you refine your responses to impress your interviewer. The more you can connect with your interviewers on an emotional level, the better your chances are they will ultimately buy your product and choose you as the best candidate.

To do this, create a unique tag line, a selling point that will make you more memorable than your competition. But, be careful you don't make the mistake of regurgitating your entire life story. Stick to what is relevant to your future employer. Too often I have seen job candidates spew everything to the interviewer and not give them an opportunity for follow-up.

You want to leave them interested and allow them the opportunity to ask follow-up questions. Stick to communicating your major career milestones and accomplishments.

Your elevator speech should be no more than a few minutes and should have three parts.

1. Part one is your opening and should be limited to two sentences. Your goal is to provide a high level overview of who you are and what you can deliver.

In the first sentence, you should incorporate key words from the job posting that the company indicated were requirements. For example, "I am a seasoned professional with 'X' years of experience successfully working with high growth companies similar to your company."

Your second sentence should explain the problem and solution you are best positioned to solve. The structure you should use is "I help _____, solve _____, by _____." Such as: I help family owned businesses solve their technology issues by implementing best-in class software. Or I help large public companies solve their profitability issues by implementing new financial metrics to more effectively manage their organization.

This structure should keep you focused on exactly how you can add tremendous value to the organization.

2. The second part is the body and should cover no more than three main points. This will prevent you from having your interviewer cut you off or worse, lose interest. Here you should provide examples where you have solved similar problems the company is currently facing.

3. Finally, wrap up your elevator speech with a recommendation to improve the company. This will help you establish credibility and authority to dominate your competition. Also, it will show that you have researched the company and are able to take initiative.

MASTERING THE ART OF SMALL TALK

How confident are you at mastering a conversation with a complete stranger? At the beginning of most interviews, job seekers resort to discussing easy topics such as the weather, sports, or traffic. However, if you start down this path, you won't be memorable. An advanced technique to help you immediately build rapport is to scan their office for pictures or certifications that they are most proud of and use that to guide your topic of conversation. Or you can use the information you gathered from their social media sites.

Did you check out my social media profiles before buying this book? If not, I would truly value connecting with you to help you continue your personal development at www.Linkedin.com/in/jerryratigan.

I had an interview once with a corporate executive who had a picture of himself completing a marathon. I brought is up at the very beginning of the interview as I was able to relate my running experience and marathon training. After we finished talking about running, I noticed a change both in the interviewer and myself. I had established that I was likable and friendly, and the interviewer felt comfortable with me. You too have the potential to connect with the interviewer on a more personal basis. Preparation and observation skills are what will help you gain an unfair advantage against your competition.

DEVELOP MEMORABLE INTERVIEW QUESTIONS

You must make yourself memorable. Creating and asking great questions are important because this confirms to your interviewer that you are seriously interested in the job. It also shows that you've been actively listening. This is a major challenge faced in your communication. Make sure that you actively listen and can talk back in terms the interviewers understand.

Whatever you do, avoid saying you don't have any questions when asked if you have any questions. If you respond to your interviewer saying you don't have any question you are making a fatal mistake. Why you ask? Because it immediately turns off your interviewer and makes them believe you are disinterested in the role. Even worse, it shows that you can't be bothered to gain a deeper understanding of the company, industry, or department issues.

During one interview, I met separately with five employees of the company. By the fourth interview, all my questions and concerns had been sufficiently answered. However, in interview four and five, I didn't tell them I was out of questions. Instead, I asked the same exact questions I asked in my earlier interviews. I even brought up the answers provided to me by the other interviewers to show how well I was listening. This worked well as I presented myself as a curious problem solver with deep interest in understanding the business.

If you want to be remembered, then be sure to ask a personal question. Here is an example that you should utilize. Based on your experience, what are some of the key characteristics to be a successful team member? Hopefully, your interviewer will open up and share information that isn't widely communicated on the exact steps you can take to be successful in your dream job.

CLOSING

The ending of the interview is also critically important. You must perfect your close and exit. Make sure you ask about next steps. When you finish with each interviewer, you could say, "Well, what can I expect to happen in this interview process? When should I expect to hear back from a recruiter? What should I do to help expedite the process?"

EXECUTION WILL SET YOU APART

Now it's time to PRACTICE! Let's implement the key lessons you have learned.

When your time comes to interview for your dream job, will you be ready? You should know that you don't want your dream interview to be your first interview. I recommend you line up a few mock interviews with your college career center or professional association to practice.

Even if you are a seasoned professional or corporate executive you may need a refresher course to get any rust off your interviewing skills. So you, too, need practice interviews.

For those newly or soon to be college graduates who have recently attended a career fair who are now attempting to land your first professional job, you may have many interviews lined up in a short period of time. In these situations, you shouldn't schedule your first choice of employer for your first interview. Think of this time period with multiple interviews similar to a sports season. Every sports league has a preseason to allow the players to practice and prepare before the actual results count. To refine your interview skills, you need a preseason.

You will want to go through the actual process, so when it matters most, you are perfectly comfortable, are familiar with being put on the spot in answering tough interview questions, know how to ask appropriate questions, know how to read the interviewer to gauge how he or she feels you're doing, and you can alter your approach when you feel the interviewer is no longer interested. The more practice you get the better. Remember a great interview should feel like a normal conversation. It should not be one-sided. So ensure the quantity and quality of questions you prepare are appropriate for the type of interview and for the person you are interviewing with.

CHAPTER 7

9 Success Tips to Ace Your Dream Job Interview

"The future belongs to those who believe
in the beauty of their dreams."

—*Eleanor Roosevelt*

MANY JOB CANDIDATES falsely assume they are prepared for their dream job interview. But, there are nine critical components you must master to guarantee a successful interview and WOW your interviewer! From my personal experience, knowing what to do and actually doing it are two completely different things.

As you read this chapter, I challenge you to evaluate yourself at each step.

1. SMILE

Now for a moment, I want you to think about the psychology of an interviewer. During your interview, they are thinking about whether you are the right fit for the company's culture and for their team. Are you someone they want working for them? They're also thinking about how you will handle meeting tight deadlines and the increased stress of new challenges. You need to present yourself as someone they will be comfortable spending lots of time with at work. Otherwise, you risk not being considered for the next step in the process.

Since you often spend more time with the people you work with than with your own family, it is crucial that the interviewer likes you. The interviewer understands there may be times you will be asked to work 10, 12, 14 hour days to meet an important deadline. You must show that you can help create a positive work environment. In order to show them you can do this, you need to be likeable. One easy thing to do is smile. While it is easy, it's often forgotten as a critical component of the interview process.

Early in my interview career, this was something I never focused on. I never gave it the attention it deserved, and it ultimately became a barrier I had to overcome. One interview I had went so smoothly I felt confident that I would land the offer. Before I left the on-site interview, the HR Director brought me into her office to give me feedback. This was a rare occurrence as in-person feedback immediately after an interview is rarely given directly to job candidates.

The number one concern shared by multiple interviewers, whom I met with that day, was that I didn't smile. Her comment caught me by surprise. I immediately thought she was joking, but she wasn't. Smiling was something that I never even considered as a potential interview flaw. I just assumed that I was natural at smiling. It was eye-awakening to learn that just the act of smiling goes far to promote yourself as likable and a viable job candidate.

Smile throughout the interview when you're answering questions. Also, when you are listening. You want to smile to show your engagement with the interviewer. Be sure that your outward appearance is open and inviting. Smiling is one way that you can achieve that.

2. SHAKE WITH POWER

Another often overlooked component of every interview is your handshake. Don't make the mistake of taking your handshake for granted. Are you absolutely confident your handshake is strong? Seriously, I'm not joking. I'm absolutely serious. Have you ever experienced an awkward handshake? Don't worry. I have an easy to tip you can implement to ensure each and every handshake you give is high quality.

Are you ready? First, grab a partner. As you begin to lean over and extend your right arm, make an effort to extend your thumb straight up in the air. This should be a slightly more exaggerated movement to you; however, no one will ever notice. Then, as your palm makes contact with the other person, let the other person close their grip first. The #1 mistake I see made over and over is people close their grips too soon, resulting in a weak handshake. Implementing this new technique will guarantee you'll have a strong handshake!

3. BE ASSERTIVE

To be considered a top candidate, you need to demonstrate a certain level of assertiveness during the interview. A misstep I experienced early in my career was during an interview with a CFO. He was a great salesman, and I was captured by his love for the products and industry. He spent almost the entire interview sharing stories about the company's growth strategies for the future. I left the interview thinking I did a fantastic job, and I would receive an offer. But, then I waited and waited and waited and waited and waited some more.

The offer never came. I was shocked and extremely disappointed. After a few weeks, I reached out to the HR Director for feedback. She told me that I did not demonstrate assertiveness in my interview with the CFO. Initially, I was disappointed and frustrated with myself. I needed to re-evaluate my interview performance. It took me some time to dust myself off and gain back my confidence in interviews with senior executives.

From this experience, I learned that certain interviewers can sometimes dominate an entire interview, and that it is the responsibility of the job candidate to speak up and be assertive in order to communicate your value to the company. Don't be afraid to jump in and take charge at certain times in the interview. Research shows companies place higher value on employees who are able to take action to get things accomplished. Before your interview ends, you must make sure you have sufficiently addressed all of the interviewers' major concerns.

4. STRATEGIC LISTENING

Listening is easy. However, being an active and engaged listener is challenging, especially during an interview. Do not formulate your response to a question while an interviewer is still talking. If you do, you risk losing focus on the interviewer and what he or she is communicating. When you are thinking of the next things you want to say, you are not fully present in the moment. Instead, pay attention to the specific language that the interviewer is using. Are there key words or phrases he or she continues to use? If you are able to use his or her own words in your responses, you will connect with your interviewer on a deeper, subconscious level.

You should show an authentic interest in the interviewer. This can be achieved by using appropriate body language. In addition to smiling, you should make eye contact between 60–70% of the time and nod your head at key points made by the interviewer. Go even further by sitting up straighter or even on the edge of your chair when he or she makes key points about the role and responsibilities. To further indicate you are listening, you should also use confirming language (I.e. uh-huh, yes, of course) to confirm you are interested in and able to comprehend the information the interviewer is conveying. By being a strategic listener, you will definitely stand out from other job candidates.

5. COMPETENT COMMUNICATOR

How you communicate determines your job interview success! To land your dream job, you must possess the skills to speak clearly, confidently, and in a moment's notice. As you speak, your responses should be organized and flow well.

In your answers, be sure to demonstrate exactly how you can fulfill the requirements of the job. To gain an unfair advantage from your competition, you need to provide detailed examples of your relevant accomplishments. A common interview mistake is for a job seeker to ramble on and on and on and on and eventually go off-topic, never completely addressing the original question. You can easily prevent this from happening to you if you stick to communicating a maximum of three main points for each response. Be sure to highlight your previous experience and how the skills you have developed can help the company.

Practice makes perfect. I recommend you practice answering interview questions by timing yourself. Give yourself only a few minutes to answer each question. If you spend more than two minutes on any single question, you may lose the interviewers' interest. Practicing helps ensure you stay within the time limit, and it also helps you formulate a structured response.

As you practice, be sure to practice pausing before you speak. This will give you a moment to gain your composure and take a full breath. After a pause, you should follow the same structure for each answer: directly answer the question with an affirmation and include a restatement of the question in your own words; and then provide a relevant work project example that gives the interviewers enough sufficient details that they feel confident you can do the job. If you want to land your dream job, you should invest more time on this subject and practice in a live environment.

I recommend you visit a Toastmasters' chapter near you. Go to www.toastmasters.org. Toastmasters is a global non-profit organization dedicated to fostering a positive and safe learning environment to build your communication skills. For a small investment, you can join a local chapter. This is one of the best ways to prepare for your interview as a component of every Toastmaster meeting is having members practice impromptu speaking. By regularly participating, you will be more confident and skilled at being able to think on your feet. This will be especially beneficial to you during your interview when the interviewer asks you a question you had not prepared for.

6. ADVANCE MIRRORING TECHNIQUES

These techniques will help you connect with your interviewers on a deeper level. On a subconscious level. Take a moment and think of your most meaningful relationship: with your best friend, a loving family member, or significant other. Now recall the last interaction you had in person. How was your communication style and your body language? Most likely your body language was open and inviting.

You might be surprised that you were copying the exact body position of the other person. Can you remember if you both were holding your arms in the same way or maybe your hand gestures were similar? For sure, I'd bet that your legs and feet were facing each other. During your interview, you can use these techniques to gain an unfair advantage over other job seekers.

First, a word of caution. Do not go overboard and mirror 100% of every change in body position or gesture your interviewer makes. If you do, you will come across as extraordinarily awkward. The interviewer will pick up on it, and it will definitely make him or her uncomfortable. Maybe even uncomfortable enough not to hire you.

So, what can you do? After you introduce yourself, shake hands, and smile, you should begin to observe how the interviewers are positioned. Are they leaning one way or the other? How are their hands placed? What about their feet? How far away from the table are they? What other body language movements can you observe?

As you get more comfortable and confident, you can make your first attempt to mirror their body language. Instead of mirroring their entire body, start off subtly. Maybe you start to mirror just their hand movements or where their arm is in relation to the chair or table. Maybe their right hand is on their armrest or maybe their right elbow is on their armrest. Try and mirror this position. Also, when you do change into a new position, hold that position for a few moments to not bring attention to what you are doing. As a guide, wait at least two or three questions before changing body positions again.

To be able to implement mirroring body language techniques, you need to be extremely prepared in your interview. The risk you should avoid is adding unnecessary stress that may negatively impact your performance. If you do plan to use this advanced body language interview tactic, be smooth and natural. You might want to practice before implementing for the first time in your interview.

As an alternative training environment, the next time you watch TV, observe the body language of the actors. What can you learn from their movements? For a more relevant training environment, use your workplace as your testing ground. At your next team or department meeting, spend more time focused on observing the body language of your colleagues. Even start to practice mirroring tactics on your team members more than what you normally do. See how you feel in that situation. Does the other person react more positively than normal? If you are able to master this skill, it will set you apart from your competition.

7. REMARKABLE STORYTELLING

The best interviewees are storytellers. If you haven't interviewed in a long while, then it is likely you are very rusty. You may even fall victim to the mistakes made by the majority of candidates: giving either short answers that don't give many details or going overboard and discussing non-relevant information. To fix this, you need to understand the components of a good story. There must be an interesting setting, sufficient edge of the seat action, a hero, a villain, and of course, an unexpected plot twist.

In your interview preparation, you want to develop mini-stories of at least five professional accomplishments. These five accomplishments do not have to all be world-class amazing record setting awards. They can be, but most candidates can be successful with accomplishments such as meeting an extreme deadline or performance target, or receiving special customer service recognition. The main objective is that you want to have a sufficient database of stories that you can immediately refer to during the interview.

When the interviewer asks you a question like "Tell me about a time you exceeded expectations," you should be able to refer to one of the stories you have prepared. First, start with the setting. Give a quick overview of the time and place. Then give a short summary of the characters involved. Next, discuss the immense challenge or dastardly villain that had to be defeated. Lastly, and most important, share how you became the hero of the story and describe the plot twists you had to endure in order to achieve the unimaginable goal.

Each answer you give should follow this format. However, you may be limited in time, so do vary how in-depth you go into each story. A good rule of thumb is to stick to two to three minutes for your response and allow for the interviewer to ask additional questions about your story. Be sure the story relates directly to a relevant job responsibility the company requires. If you use these guidelines, your storytelling ability will immediately improve and will give you an unfair advantage against your competition.

8. ADVANCED NOTE TAKING

Job candidates miss the opportunity to take notes during the interview. In every interview, make sure you bring a compendium with a few resumes. Just showing up to the interview with your compendium shows that you are prepared and are taking the interview seriously. During the interview, you should only take brief notes and only when the interviewers are sharing very important information. This will show the interviewer you are very engaged.

Another benefit to taking notes is it allows you the chance to list out key words and industry jargon the interviewers are using which you can refer to later in your responses. This also helps if you may have multiple interviews on the same day. In these situations, you are going to have a challenging time developing remarkable follow-up questions and summaries of your interview if you did not take notes. Those candidates who took notes will have a distinct advantage to recall key information discussed during the interview to create outstanding thank you messages.

9. ASK FOR THE JOB

Many interviewees fail to implement a key negotiation strategy at the very end of their interview. Surprisingly and to their detriment, they never actually ask for the job. Do not make this common mistake. You should ask for the job even though it may not feel natural. You may not view yourself as a salesperson, and that is all right. Most professionals do not consider themselves to be good salesman. Unfortunately, you do need to implement some salesman tactics as you are selling YOU!

One way to ensure you get an offer for your dream job is to have your conclusion memorized. For example, you could say, "Mr. or Ms. Interviewer, I believe that I've demonstrated to you that I'm an ideal fit for your team and company. I possess the skills and experience to be successful in this role. You should hire me."

By asking for the job, you are planting the seed that will change how the interviewers view you. Potentially, they may start brainstorming ideas of projects you will be working on or tasks you will be assigned. Putting your interviewers in this new mindset is a real asset to you. Don't miss an opportunity that the majority of candidates are not taking full advantage of.

SUMMARY

Learn from my mistakes, and the mistakes of other job candidates. In your next interview, when you are preparing for your dream job, think of this wisdom that can help you eliminate interview missteps. Remember to apply these tips during you next interview. First smile and deliver a strong handshake. Then breathe magnificently and strategically listen. Demonstrate advance mirroring techniques while being an assertive, passionate storyteller. Don't forget to take notes. And, finally ask for the job.

CHAPTER 8

How to Master the Online Interview!

*"Science and technology revolutionize our lives,
but memory, tradition and myth frame our response."*

—*Arthur Schlesinger*

ARE YOU READY to ride the spectacular wave of innovation to land your dream job? Your next job could be right down the street, in the nearby state, or even halfway around the world. Today, more and more companies are utilizing technology to make their job fulfillment process more effective and less costly. Employers can now recruit potential employees from anywhere in the world for any job and across all industries.

The same use of technology can be leveraged by job seekers. You now possess limitless ability to interview for any company in any location in the world. I have used online interviews to obtain a job in Australia while living in the U.S. on two separate occasions. From those experiences, I have created a blueprint to master the online interview using Skype, GoToMeeting, or any other online interview tool.

I've been on both sides of the online interview process. As a job seeker, I've had to wake up in the middle of the night to make an online interview; I've interviewed in an empty apartment the week before I was departing Australia on my way back to the U.S.; and I've even interviewed for a job in Miami, Florida, while in Borneo, Malaysia. As an interviewer, I've interviewed job candidates from shockingly expensive corporate boardrooms to make-shift offices that were thrown together last minute. Based on my unique perspective, I've created an easy to follow step-by-step process that you can easily implement to perform your best.

Let's begin with your attitude and mindset. You cannot and should not underestimate the online interview. You may assume that interviewing online is the same as a regular on-site interview. If you hold this belief, you are mistaken. While it is just as important as the in-person interview, it is possibly more challenging. Why? Mainly because there are many more factors that you must account for that you wouldn't otherwise.

So take note of the factors you need consider and prepare for, and you will be successful:

TECHNOLOGY

Don't make the mistake of assuming everything will go as smoothly as planned without checking and double checking your computer and software. Dealing with technology issues immediately before the interview could derail you. If you experience preventable technology mishaps, the interviewers may not consider you a viable candidate. So, make sure to give yourself adequate time to test your system, which will prevent many technology issues.

You must be aware of how the other person sees you on his or her screen. Therefore, you should perform a test run paying attention to what the other person will see. And, check your settings at least thirty minutes prior to the interview, ideally the day before. If you have Skype, you can go into settings to test your picture and microphone.

You can make sure that the adjustments on the screen are appropriate. You don't want to start the interview looking really strange because you are too close to the screen making it uncomfortable for your interviewer. But, you also don't want to be too far away, or then the interviewer will see the ceiling and only the top of your head.

Make sure to run a mic check. Testing one . . . two. Testing one . . . two . . . three. You will want to make sure that you talk slightly slower and louder than you would normally speak in a normal conversation because the person on the other side may not have their speaker turned up. To make sure the volume is clear, you should ask before the interview officially starts if the interviewer can hear you sufficiently. This will be your only opportunity to catch significant sound issues. If your speaker is too far away from your computer, this could be an issue. Also, you may want to consider using a headset or external microphone if your computer microphone is unreliable.

Finally, make sure you have access to a power outlet and high-speed internet. I was in an interview once where my Wi-Fi connection was intermittent. My connection was poor, and at times, I could not understand what the interviewer was saying. Consequently, I had to ask him to repeat himself, and I could tell he was becoming a bit frustrated as the interview went on. In order to avoid constantly asking him to repeat himself, I had to guess what was being said. I didn't want him to get more frustrated and hold the poor connection against me. This was not the ideal situation so do try and connect to a land line or move as close to your Wi-Fi connection as possible. Do not let technology sabotage your online interview.

LOCATION, BACKGROUND AND LIGHTING

Where will you be for the online interview? Do you have a home office? If not, you will need to be creative to come up with an alternative option. The location should be quiet; clean; and most importantly, somewhere that you feel comfortable. It should be somewhere where you won't get distracted. A few times I interviewed at home while my son was a baby. Looking back on those interviews, I put myself at risk as his noise could have distracted both me and my interviewer. So if you are at home with a family going about their day-to-day activities and you have a critical interview, you might want to negotiate with them to not be home during your interview.

A word of caution. You may feel compelled to use an empty office at your current place of employment, but do not make this choice as you risk someone inadvertently seeing you, which would put you in an awkward situation with your current employer. Also, public places like Starbucks are not recommended as you cannot control the noise, and you may be constantly interrupted by other customers. If you are struggling to locate a quiet space, consider finding a quiet room at your public library or community center. A last resort could be finding a shared office space business where you can rent an office for an hour or half day.

Once you've determined your location, you will need to evaluate your background and lighting needs. These are two controllable elements of the online interview you should address. A recommended first step is to open up Skype on your computer to view how you will actually look to your interviewer. You will want to make sure you are in front of a wall that is free from clutter and wall hangings that could distract your interviewer.

Is your lighting sufficient? What time of day is your interview? Does your room have natural light you can take advantage of? If not, or if the lighting quality is not sufficient, you should add a floor lamp or two to the area you will be interviewing in. Think of these tasks as you are creating your very own personal interview studio.

You do not need to go out and buy the most expensive lighting equipment; however, you'll want to make sure you present yourself in the highest quality picture as possible. I had a friend once hire a professional lighting company to set up a temporary studio in her home office as she was very determined to be seen at her very best. But for less than $20, you can go to your local hardware or department store such as Home Depot or Lowes in the U.S. or Big W or Bunnings in Australia.

Also, for those of you who wear eye glasses, you may experience a glare issue. I've had to deal with this situation, which took me many interviews to finally solve. In some of my online interviews, I noticed that my glasses had significant glare on them from the lights. This caused me to stress out, worrying that the glare was too overwhelming for the interviewer to deal with.

I grew more concerned and my stress level continued to rise. I did not want it to be an issue and possibly be a distraction to my interviewer. Fortunately, I can still see without my eye glasses, so I decided last minute not to wear them. However, in all my online interviews after that, I did wear my eye glasses as I set aside enough preparation time to adjust my lighting to eliminate this interview obstacle. You too can solve your background and lighting challenges if you give yourself sufficient preparation time.

YOU'RE GOING TO WEAR WHAT?

How you look matters! Studies show you are more likely to get hired if you look well-groomed. Psychologists call this pattern the halo effect: where you take one aspect of somebody, such as their good looks, as a proxy for their overall character. So what can you do to make the odds more in your favor?

Dress to impress! Follow the same guidelines in the previous chapter; however, with an online interview, you will also need to make sure your clothes are not washed out by your background. For example, if the wall behind you in the interview is white, then I'd recommend not wearing a white shirt. You will want to have some contrast between you and your background in order to present your best self. Another option is to get feedback before the online interview. You could take a picture from your computer showcasing how you will look to the interviewer and send it to a friend for feedback.

For an online interview, you can get away with wearing shorts and no shoes since that part of your person will not be seen on screen. This way you can be comfortable, but still appear professional. Make sure to use caution, but you do have additional freedom that you don't have during an on-site interview. I've interviewed a few times in a shirt, tie, sports coat, shorts and sandals, resulting in no visible difference in my performance. Lastly, give thought to control any shine and cover up any major blemishes.

MOCK INTERVIEW

Similar to an in person interview, you should never schedule the first online interview you have for your dream job. Do take the time to plan a practice online interview to get more comfortable with the process. The old saying that practice makes perfect is very applicable. You want to be able to touch, feel, and experience the actual process, so that you are extremely confident with low stress when it counts the most. What can you do? Ask a close friend or family member to put you in the hot seat and test your system. Schedule a short practice interview with them just to receive honest and timely feedback on everything you have learned.

EYE CONTACT

You want to demonstrate the right kind of eye contact that exudes confidence. So make sure you balance the time you look directly into your interviewer's eyes and when you look away. You definitely do not want to stare at him or her, but you also need to show that you have the self-worth to stay engaged with your interviewer. To reduce the strange feeling of looking directly into the camera, put a small picture directly above the camera to keep your eyes focused. You may want to give this a try in your mock interviews to see if this would benefit you.

USING NOTES

Unique to any online interview is that you have the opportunity to use notes and not be concerned that it will have any negative impact on your credibility. However, you must spend enough time during your preparation to organize your notes, so your interviewer does not know you are using them. You should have your resume readily available as well as the notes that you have researched on the company and the interviewer. During the interview when you look away, you can scan the notes to make sure that you're covering all your key points and ask the right questions you've painstakingly prepared.

Your prime real estate is on both sides of your computer. If used effectively, you can use the screen of your computer that isn't directly visible to your interviewer. I've even taped a few index cards I had with specific items I needed to discuss on the top of my laptop. You could even set up an easel behind your computer if you feel you need the additional space. A word of caution is that all these notes should be supplementary cues for you to easily recall critical information. It should not eliminate your preparation time; you still need to prepare your answers and memorize your resume.

Will you accept my challenge to implement all of these critical components to your next online interview? Leverage technology, present yourself in the best light, dress to impress, practice, maintain eye contact, and take effective notes. If you do these things, you can be successful and land that dream job you deserve.

CHAPTER 9

Seal the Deal to Land
Your Dream Job!

*"Diligent follow-up and follow-through will set you apart
from the crowd and communicate excellence."*

—John Maxwell

TOO OFTEN I have seen ideal candidates miss out on landing their dream offer because they didn't follow up appropriately, and shockingly, sometimes not at all. Throughout my own interviews, I have always utilized standard follow-up procedures to ensure I didn't miss out on an offer I had within my grasp.

The follow-up process begins when you're wrapping up your final interview of the day. Sometimes this interview could be with the hiring managers, their boss, or possibly someone from HR.

CLOSING QUESTIONS

When the interviewer asks if you have any final questions, be sure to ask these two questions: "What are the next steps in the process," and "Do you have any concerns I have not addressed?"

By asking these two questions, you have a chance to gain insider information about the company's hiring timetable. It also gives you the opportunity to receive immediate feedback, which is very important. Since you are still in the interview, you may have the opportunity to fix or explain certain issues the interviewer may have. Based on the interviewers' answers to these two important questions, you will get an understanding of whether or not you did well, and if you should expect to progress through the interview process to the next stage.

If the interviewers' responses are vague when you ask what the next steps are in the interview process that is a red flag. For example if they tell you, "We're in the process of bringing in many candidates, you should hear back from HR in the next couple of weeks," this is code for you won't be receiving an offer. With the second question, if they begin to raise additional concerns or they bring up other issues you thought you addressed, then you have more work to do. At that moment, there may be one final opportunity for you to sell yourself. Immediately, you need to revisit your interview responses to understand where you may have gone off track.

To help put it in perspective, let's compare this to purchasing a car. When was the last time you bought a car? How many different dealerships did you visit? When you were asked by the salesperson to make the final purchase, did you say yes immediately? Or did you say you needed more time to think about it? A good salesperson may have continued the sales conversation in an attempt to overcome all of your undisclosed objections. Maybe you thought the price was too high, safety features were too low, or the warranty was insufficient. Unless the salesperson kept you interested and they actively listened to your concerns, it is unlikely you bought that car from them.

In your interview, you need to take on the mindset of a great salesperson. Your number one priority before you leave the interview is to identify any remaining objections that the interviewer may still have to hiring you. A question I use is "are there any other concerns you have about my resume or experience that I have not sufficiently addressed." The response to this question gives me a good idea of whether I am likely to continue on in the hiring process.

On the other hand, if your interviewer tells you they were impressed and they're going to recommend that you are advanced to the next round, you will know you did well. They may even ask you to interview more that day to help the company be more efficient in their hiring process. I've been on both sides of this situation too, as interviewee and interviewer. Being flexible is a key characteristic to being successful when this occurs.

FOLLOW-UP EMAIL

No matter how you finalize your interview, before you leave, make sure you obtain contact information so you can follow up with all of your interviewers. Ideally, you want to obtain their business cards so you have their contact information, including their email. Email is the best line of communication as handwritten notes may not get there in time.

It is standard practice to send a thank you email to each of your interviewers within 24 hours. I recommend you go one step further and really make your email stand out. Invest the time to describe how you appreciated their time, bring up a key job requirement they specifically mentioned during the interview, and reiterate how excited you are to join their team. Make sure to highlight your key deliverables that can best add value to the company and address any concerns that may have been left unanswered during the interview. This will demonstrate you were paying attention. There is no need to write a thesis, two or three paragraphs is absolutely fine.

Now that you've sent your thank you email, what do you do next? Do you remember how I had you start tracking all of your applications in excel? Now is the time for you to go back to your spreadsheet and update your job search status for this specific application. You should have a column indicating you sent out a thank you note. The more organized you are, the more you stay on top of each application's current status, and the less stressed you will be during your job search.

THE WAIT WAIT WAIT WAIT WAIT

After you've sent the thank you note and updated your status for this job in your application tracker, it is time to wait. I recommend waiting three to four days after your final interview to initiate your next contact. If no one from the company has contacted you, then it is advisable to send a short status update email just to check in and communicate that you are still very interested in the job.

Your objective is to keep your application in the front of their minds during their hiring process. Once you send an email, if you don't get a response within one day, then I would pick up the phone and call your HR contact. Be cautious not to seem too anxious or desperate in your email or voicemail. If you send too many messages in a short period after your interview, the company may identify your anxious behavior as a possible red flag.

If you are using an external recruiter, then this approach will be modified. In this situation, you should take more initiative and follow up with the recruiter earlier in the process, possibly, even immediately after the interview. It is likely your recruiter is going to reach out to their contact at the company to find out how you did the same day you interview.

I actually have had interviews using a recruiter where immediately after the interview, I called the recruiter and shared my feedback. Within the next hour, they reached out to the company, and by the end of the day, they contacted me back to give me an assessment of whether or not I was moving on to the next round and if I could expect an offer. When you are not using a recruiter, it is more challenging to obtain timely feedback regarding where you stand in the recruitment process as you have no direct link to the company that is working on your behalf.

In situations where you feel the hiring process is dragging on endlessly, the company may have given an offer to another candidate and that individual has not yet accepted. You may be the plan B or C candidate so they want to keep you in the process as a viable candidate. The company is buying more time by not getting back to you until they get a decision from their plan A or B candidates.

If more than a week goes by without hearing a response, then the company has most likely moved on. In this situation, I would make one last attempt to contact HR and ask for feedback. Were you not confident? Did you come across as anxious? Did you not clearly articulate your skills to match the job description? Did you not ask appropriate questions? These are all things that you can learn from.

If you are able to discover what key criteria you didn't meet, then you'll be able to practice more and improve during your next interview.

Waiting on the job offer is both very exciting and stressful. After implementing these expert tips, be sure to take time to debrief and assess your interviewing process. Also, take time to celebrate your accomplishment as you have come a long way. Ideally, the next time you hear from the company I hope you hear, "we'd like to make you an offer!"

CHAPTER 10

Negotiate Your Way to
Higher Compensation

*"You must never try to make all the money
that's in a deal. Let the other fellow make some money too,
because if you have a reputation for always making all
the money, you won't have many deals."*

—*J. Paul Getty*

WHEN YOU RECEIVE a job offer, do not accept the first offer. Make sure to negotiate! You deserve to get paid what you are worth. Research shows candidates who negotiate receive higher total compensation including salary, bonus, and number of vacation days. Negotiation is definitely a learned skill, and something I've had significant experience with during my career. For certain roles, I went back and forth with the company many times during the negotiation process. What I have learned is the more expertise you have, the more negotiation power you have.

In order to receive a higher salary even before negotiating, you must know the primary factors that companies use to develop a salary range for job candidates: years of experience, education level, and professional certifications. I highly recommend you research and obtain a certification that is widely recognized and valued in your industry. For accounting and finance professionals, the most common advanced certifications include CPA, certified public accountant; CMA, certified management accountant; and CIA, certified internal auditor. I have attained the CPA and CMA certifications. By having these globally recognized credentials, more job opportunities became available to me and have helped me achieve a higher compensation level than I would have without those certifications.

WHEN TO NEGOTIATE

For those of you entering the workforce for the first time or are a young professional, you should wait to negotiate until your final interview or when you get a call back from the HR department saying they want to extend you an offer. However, if you are a seasoned professional or corporate executive, salary is normally discussed during the HR screening interview. In this situation, you can expect to be asked either what your salary expectation is and/or what your current salary is.

The company will ask these questions because they want to ensure there isn't a significant salary expectation gap that cannot be reconciled. It is in both your interests, the company's and yours, to find out if it is worth the time and effort for you to continue in the process. Interestingly, there is a movement to prevent employers from asking about current salary in the interview process. This is a topic to continue to monitor as it will require a different negotiation approach for you to execute. If you are working with an external recruiter, then you should discuss your range of compensation in your first meeting in order to set clear expectations.

KNOW THE RANGE OF COMPENSATION

If you aren't working with a recruiter before beginning your negotiations, you need to know the appropriate range of compensation. You can solve this mystery by researching salary benchmarks for your experience level and industry.

A great source is Robert Half, a global recruiting and research firm. I've used their guides as a starting point for all my salary negotiations. Their research is categorized by level and title, from a new professional just leaving university all the way up to the executive or partner level. Another credible salary study is from the Institute of Management Accountants. They put together a global research report, taking your years of relevant experience and number of professional certifications to calculate a compensation range you could expect to earn.

TIPS FOR NEGOTIATING A HIGHER SALARY

To gain the highest possible salary you must establish your value. When beginning the salary negotiation do not give your number first, as it has the possibility to scare off your prospective employer. Instead, aim to learn their budget limitations for the position. Ask them if they could share that information with you. Also, ask what factors were involved in determining that figure. Getting their framework will allow you to better position yourself to overcome certain subjective factors. It also will prevent you from disclosing a number that is significantly outside of that range.

If the Company shares an amount or a range, first acknowledge them for sharing that information with a reserved thank you. Try and not react favorably to their first offer. By showing some disappointment, the Company may be inclined to raise their offer as they want to hire a motivated employee. A response I've used to increase the offer, is to respond with tempered disappointment. For example, "Thank you. I am grateful for the offer and can see myself being successful as an employee at "_____". However, by accepting that salary I wouldn't feel the Company values my skills and experience. I would be happier to join at a more fair salary of $x. Last, be sure to conclude your counter offer by reiterating the monumental business problems you will solve.

NEGOTIATING OTHER THINGS BESIDES SALARY

In some cases, salary may not be negotiable, depending on if you are working at a large company with set salary ranges for specific job categories. In these circumstances, you should still have some ability to negotiate your eligible bonus and other compensation items. I dealt with this situation when I graduated college and started my first full-time professional position. The company I worked for had very restrictive salary ranges and all new hires with the same degree received the same salary. Once I learned it wasn't an option to negotiate a higher salary, I got creative and was able to negotiate a higher sign-on bonus. Be creative when you are negotiating to give yourself the highest probability of success.

You can negotiate many things: your title, signing bonus, annual bonus, time when your next salary review will be performed, number of vacation days, ability to work remotely, car allowance, continuing education, travel, and many more. In any negotiation, you want to create a short list of items that you care about the most and focus specifically on obtaining those.

If you negotiate each and every single compensation item the company offers, then there is risk that the company applies a brick wall strategy. You do not want the company to abruptly end negotiations, telling you to take it or leave it. My initial focus has always included salary, bonus, and vacation days. For the other items, once I was an employee of the company, I would re-negotiate these items in my next compensation review.

SUMMARY

You now are empowered with information to negotiate the compensation for your dream job. You must be prepared by arming yourself with timely and relevant benchmark information. And, whatever you do, don't accept the company's first offer. Negotiate!

Obtain your FREE Salary Negotiation Resource Guide at:

www.AcedInterview.com/bonus

CHAPTER 11

Overcoming the Pain and Suffering of Job Search Fatigue

"I've failed over and over and over again in my life and that is why I succeed."

—Michael Jordan (Basketball Legend and Billionaire)

I F YOU FEEL overwhelmed, discouraged, disappointed, or burnt out from the job searching process, don't fret; there is hope. You may have filled out numerous applications, attended countless networking events, and now aren't quite sure how you should spend your time. You may feel like your confidence is shattered, causing you to feel less motivated and energetic while applying for more jobs and performing the necessary follow-up activities. Additionally, companies and interviewers may now sense your lost interest, creating a red flag. But, there is hope.

I've been in your shoes. I've hit major speed bumps and road blocks interviewing all throughout my career. I've not only been burnt out, I have even become depressed. In a few job searches, I definitely lost my momentum and kindred spirit. I've been exactly where you are. I've experienced the pain and worthlessness you feel when you send off your resume to companies never to hear back again. I've also experienced my fair share of rejection. It was all right. You will be all right. I want to use the knowledge I've gained to provide you with needed inspiration. You can still achieve your goal of landing your dream job. It's just going to be more difficult.

CHANGE YOUR MINDSET

Remember your self-worth is not tied to whether or not you have a successful job search. However, it is important to recognize you're in a more delicate frame of mind when you start experiencing continuous disappointment. So, you need a change of mindset as it is likely you are focusing more on the negatives than the positive.

UPDATE AND REPOST YOUR RESUME

A simple way to achieve this is to view your job search similar to the real estate market. What if you were selling a house that's been on the market for many months? By now, it has lost its initial appeal and may start to have a stigma attached to it. Potential buyers may start asking their real estate agent why it has been on the market so long, worrying something is wrong with it.

A good real estate agent would probably recommend that the seller take it off the market, then re-list it with a different description to advertise to a different target market. Maybe the original target market was not open to receiving the message. Maybe the area the house is located has more young families moving in, but it was being advertised as a house for retirees. Alternatively, maybe the home owner needs to make needed upgrades to match the comparable houses in the area.

In any case, there are many factors impacting why a house stays on the market longer than expected. Now think of yourself as this house; then ask yourself what steps can you immediately take to reinvigorate the process and spice up your appeal to your future employer?

Do just like the real-estate agent suggests: take your resume off the job boards. Change it up if you need to, and then re-list it. With data analytics, companies and recruiters can sort through resumes to know when it was first listed and then updated. You likely were not being contacted on jobs sites because you weren't showing up in the searches. As a hiring manager, I would search only candidates who had updated their resume in the last 30 days. These candidates were more appealing solely due to being in the very early stages of their job search.

Another recommended course of action is to reposition yourself in the market and find a mentor to help you do so. You may want to do more research and meet with a few different recruiters. A few different people who have their ear to the ground, causing them to understand the changing trends in the market, may be able to open new employment doors for you.

UPSKILL YOURSELF - DEVELOP NEEDED SKILLS

In the meantime, you can start completing project work as a consultant. Or, you can reach out to companies that specialize in special short-term projects. Depending on your financial situation, maybe you could volunteer. In all of these options, you want to focus mostly on adding new skills that are in demand which you currently don't possess. Consider working on projects that will help you regain your credibility, authority, and enhance your overall expertise.

If you're able to implement some of these steps in your grueling job search process, you'll increase your volume of positive feedback and begin to regain positive momentum. If you need additional assistance, if after many months and after reformulating your plan and following the above advice, you're still facing immovable road blocks, then you may need to join a mastermind community. This may be the point where you need to surround yourself with individuals who will help change your mindset to give you a more positive outlook on your job search process.

CLOSING REMARKS

W E'VE COME A long way together. I sincerely hope the value I've delivered in this book has exceeded your expectations. If you implement this expert knowledge you will tremendously improve your chances of success to land your dream job.

May I ask that you take a moment now and leave an honest review for the book on Amazon? I'd love to hear how much this book impacted your job search process. Thanks in advance.

Now I'll leave you with an inspirational quote from Napoleon Hill:

"If you have tried and met with defeat:
if you have planned and watched your plans as they
were crushed before your eyes; just remember that the
greatest people in all history were the products of courage,
and courage, you know, is born in the cradle of adversity."

PRICELESS JOB SEACH RESOURCES

Join our ACED community and connect with other amazingly ambitious career driven professionals and like-minded experts who are changing the world. We'd love to hear from and continue to support you.

Facebook Community Group Page: Aced Interview:
www.facebook.com/groups/1200833756690892/
www.twitter.com/Aced_Interview

To obtain your FREE Audiobook and FREE Salary Negotiation Resource Guide ($39 value) please visit:

www.AcedInterview.com/bonus

ABOUT THE AUTHOR

Gerald Ratigan is a CMA, CPA (Texas) and SVP Finance, Chief Accounting Officer at MoneyOnMobile, Inc.—a global payments company publicly traded in the U.S. with operations in India.

While working for numerous Blue Chip Global Organizations across the world, he has acquired significant leadership experience in external audit, internal audit, financial reporting, budgeting, forecasting, controllership, corporate finance and IT system implementations. He has led the Accounting and Financial Reporting departments at three different public companies.

Currently, he holds leadership positions in local and regional levels within the Institute of Management Accountants and is a member of its Speaker's Bureau and Campus Influencer Program. He founded the South Florida Professional Chapter and University of Miami student chapter. In 2013, he was IMA's Young Professional of the Year.

He is an international award winning public speaker and Finance Manager for Toastmasters District 50 in Dallas, Texas. He has held numerous chapter and area leadership positions. As a chapter president he led his team to #11 in the world of over 14,000 chapter in education awards earned.

He also serves as an Executive Advisor to the Sarbanes-Oxley and Internal Controls Professional Group. He has delivered numerous SOX, Corporate Governance and Ethical Leadership presentations to all levels of management including Board of Directors and at the IMA's National Conference.

Contact him today to schedule him as an entertaining and memorable Keynote Speaker for your next event. Send an email to geraldratigan@gmail.com.

Connect with him:

On Twitter @JerryRatigan
On Linkedin at www.LinkedIn.com/in/jerryratigan
And read his insights on his blog at www.jerryratigan.com

NOTES

NOTES

Made in the USA
Las Vegas, NV
21 December 2020